Home

Home

New Arabic Poems

البيت

CALICO

© 2020 by Two Lines Press

The copyright to the individual pieces in this book remains
with the individual rightsholder or translator, unless otherwise noted.

Saadiah Mufarreh's "My Dreams Often Humble Themselves" is from *Banipal 43* (2012).

Ahmed Shafie's poems 1, 3, and 4 were published in Arabic under different numbers in *77*
(Kotob Khan, 2017). They are republished here with permission from the publisher.

Additional credits appear on page 147.

Home is second in the Calico Series.

Two Lines Press
582 Market Street, Suite 700, San Francisco, CA 94104
www.twolinespress.com

ISBN: 978-1-949641-07-3 (matte edition)

Cover design by Crisis
Typesetting and interior design by LOKI

Printed in the United States of America

Library of Congress Cataloging-in-Publication Data

NAMES: Abu Hawwash, Samer. Poems. Selections. English. |
Abu Hawwash, Samer. Poems. Selections. | Wehbe, Rawad translator.
TITLE: Home: new Arabic poems / [Samer Abu Hawwash], [and eight others];
[translated by Rawad Wehbe], [and eleven others].
DESCRIPTION: San Francisco: Two Lines Press, 2020. | In English and Arabic. |
Summary: "Poems that explore the intimate world of everyday life through
contemporary voices from across the Arabic-speaking world"-- Provided by publisher.
IDENTIFIERS: LCCN 2020007890 | ISBN 9781949641073 (trade paperback)
SUBJECTS: LCSH: Arabic poetry--20th century--Translations into English. |
Arabic poetry--21st century--Translations into English. | Arabic
poetry--20th century. | Arabic poetry--21st century.
CLASSIFICATION: LCC PJ7694.E3 H66 2020 | DDC 892.7/160803564--dc23
LC record available at https://lccn.loc.gov/2020007890

THIS BOOK WAS PUBLISHED WITH SUPPORT
FROM THE NATIONAL ENDOWMENT FOR THE ARTS.

Samer Abu Hawwash
Translated by RAWAD WEHBE
11

Iman Mersal
Two poems translated by ROBYN CRESWELL
Four poems translated by ROBIN MOGER
35

Mohamad Nassereddine
Translated by HUDA FAKHREDDINE
55

Saadiah Mufarreh
Translated by ALLISON BLECKER
63

Riyad al-Salih al-Hussein
Translated by RANA ISSA and SUNEELA MUBAYI
79

Ines Abassi
Translated by KOEN DE CUYPER
and HODNA BENTALI GHARSALLAH NUERNBERG
91

Ahmed Shafie
Translated by HODNA BENTALI GHARSALLAH NUERNBERG
and AHMED SHAFIE
111

Ashjan Hendi
Translated by MONEERA AL-GHADEER
121

Fadhil al-Azzawi
Translated by WILLIAM M. HUTCHINS
129

Contributors
139

Credits
147

Samer Abu Hawwash

Palestine

TRANSLATED BY RAWAD WEHBE

سيلفي أخيرة مع عالم يحتضر

تكفي أحياناً
وريقةُ شجرٍ مهملة،
مفتاحاً
إلى اسمٍ
يضيعُ.

One Last Selfie
with a Dying World

Sometimes, it only takes
a neglected leaf
to unlock
a name
misplaced.

يكفي
بعد أن تملأ الحمامَ بالبخار
أن تنفخَ في المرآة
كما تنفخُ في حساء ساخن
حتى تعيدَ إلى جميعِ الوجوهِ الصامتة،
في غابة رأسِك،
جميعَ أصواتِها الضائعة.

It's enough
once the bathroom fills with steam
to exhale onto the mirror
the way you'd blow on hot soup
to give back to all the silent faces
nestled in the forest of your head
their lost voices.

واقفاً أمامَ المرآة،
لا تستطيع أيضاً أن تكبتَ هذا اللهاث،
الذي يصيرُ سعاراً،
الذي لا تعرف إن كان يصدرُ عنك،
أو عن حيوان آخر
على مقربة شديدة

شديدة جداً
حتى الجِلد.

Standing before the mirror
you too cannot restrain the breathing,
which becomes feral,
unsure if it comes from you,
or from some other beast
looming beside

so close
down to the skin.

تسمعُ هديرَ حيواتٍ
تنهضُ على مقربةٍ منك،
كوبٌ يتحطمُ في مغسلةِ الجيران،
أقدامٌ صغيرةٌ تطأ الأرض،
عيونٌ تحاولُ ابتلاعَ الضوء
كأفواهِ أسماكٍ جائعة.

You hear noises hum into life
bursting nearby,
a glass shattering in the neighbor's sink,
little feet stomping the ground,
eyes trying to swallow the light
like the mouths of hungry fish.

وميضٌ
لن تحاولَ هذه المرة تفسيرَه
بالكلمات المعتادة؛
نظراتٌ عاجزةٌ
عن أن تصيرَ وجوهاً،
أياديَ عاجزةٌ
عن أن تصيرَ لمسات.

A flash
you won't bother to explain this time
using ordinary words:
glances incapable
of becoming faces,
hands short
of becoming touch.

تنظرُ إلى العالم
الذي لم يكن يوماً؛
هذا شبحٌ
يرتعشُ في خزانة الملابس،
هذا شبحٌ آخر
على طرف اللسان.

You look at the world
that never was;
this is a ghost
trembling in the wardrobe.
This is another ghost
on the tip of your tongue.

في الصباح
تعرفُ أنك ستفعل ما درج الموتى على فعله
منذ آلاف السنين،
تتذكر الخبزَ والقهوةَ وروائح أخرى
تراكمث على شال الأم أو الجدة
أو الأم والجدة معاً،
في صباحاتٍ ماضية.

Morning
You know you'll do what the dead have always done
for thousands of years.
You recall the bread, coffee, and other smells
accumulated in mother's shawl, or grandmother's,
or mingled in both
from mornings past.

تجلسُ زمناً طويلاً
—بلا زمن—
أمامَ الحذاء.
تحاولُ صداقةً مع غبار غير مرئيّ
باشرَ حياته هنا
على غفلةٍ منك.

You sit up for a while
—outside Time—
facing the shoes.
You attempt to befriend transparent dust
going about life
unbeknownst to you.

أحاولُ وأحوالُ؛
ليس في رأسي فحسب هذا الرعب؛
جالسٌ على كرسيّ المطبخ،
بين يديّ همبرغر المذبحة الضخم،
وعليّ ابتلاعه
بقضمةٍ واحدة.

I try again and again.
This terror is not only in my head:
sitting on the kitchen chair,
with a supersize burger in my hand
that I must swallow
in a single bite.

في كلّ ذرةِ غبارٍ
مذبوحٌ آخر سيأتي،
وفي مطبخ آخر
أحدهم يخوضُ نقاشاً عائلياً بسيطاً
عن نقصٍ اعتياديّ في الخبزِ
أو الماءِ،
أو المرح.

In every speck of dust
another sacrifice will arrive.
In another kitchen
one of them will enter a simple family discussion
about the customary shortage of bread,
water,
or happiness.

الناقص الحقيقيّ هو البحر.
ولكن ماذا نروي،
عن كلّ هذا الدم،
لأيدي أطفالنا
الأرقّ من الماء.

What's really missing is the sea.
But what do we tell
our children's hands
hands more delicate than water
about all this blood?

Iman Mersal

Egypt

TWO POEMS TRANSLATED
BY ROBYN CRESWELL

FOUR POEMS TRANSLATED
BY ROBIN MOGER

جرس الصباح

تنفتح العين مثل ستارة مسرح
في الظلام، تلمسُ قدمان الواقع
لا يحدثُ صحوٌ وخشبُ الأرضية له نفس حرارة الجلد
تكرار طازج وهذا يوم يُضاف إليه أو يُؤخذ منه
سيبدأ عرض ارتجاليّ عند الوصول إلى مطبخ العائلة
ربما تكون تلك القهوة السوداء هي جرس الصباح،
هكذا يستلم الواحد جائزة العودة سالماً من النوم.

Morning bell

The eye opens like a curtain rising
feet feel in the dark for something solid
nothing's awake and the floorboards are skin temperature
a fresh repetition, today will be one more or one less
an impromptu concert strikes up in the kitchen
maybe this black coffee is the morning bell
the prize you win for returning safe from sleep.

Translated by Robyn Creswell

يهدمون بيت أهلي

كأنَّ المعاولَ ليست كافيةً للهدم
باليدين،
ينزع العمالُ الشباكَ الذي اعتادت أن تتسلّل منه الجنيّات.
وبركلةٍ، يسقط البابُ الخلفيُّ إلى الخارج، تسقطُ ذاكرةُ الباب
وأدوسُ على أقماع من السكر، حبّاتٍ من البرتقال والمانجو كانت
زائرات خجولاتٌ يخبئنها تحت طُرَحِهنَّ السوداء،
كن يأتين بعد صلاة المغرب وكانت أطرافُ جلاليبهن الطويلة تلمس
عتبةَ هذا الباب.
باب الهدايا والساحرات أصبح باباً لنفسه،
والسقف الذي فشل في حماية الطفولة من أمطار الدلتا،
يعود الآن إلى أصله ؛ أشجارٌ يمكن عدّها.
يهدمون الآن غرفةَ نومها المهجورة، لتَخرجَ خصلاتٌ من شَعْرها ما
زالت مبلولةً. شعرٌ مبلولٌ يخرج من شقوق جدار طينيّ ؛
جدارٌ سيُهدم بعد دقائق ليصير كومةً من ترابٍ،
كأن أحداً لم يسند أبداً ظهرَهُ عليه.
هل تحمّمتُ أمي قبل النوم أم في الفجر؟
هل حملتُ خصلاتٍ تنتمي إليها من بين أسنان المشط خوفاً من

38

They tear down my family home

As if sledgehammers weren't enough
the demolition men use their hands
to tear down the window djinn used to flit through
and with a kick the back door—even its memory—is gone.
Underfoot I feel the remains of sugar loaf, orange pips, and the mangoes
our furtive visitors hid under black headwraps.
They would come after evening prayer, the hems of their long jalabiyas
brushing across the door's threshold
a door of gifts and sorceresses, now a door to nowhere.
The roof that never protected my childhood from the Delta rains
has reverted to its old self—a few trees you can count on one hand.
Now they're tearing down her old bedroom casting into the air
strands of her still-wet hair, hair that slips through the cracks
of earthen walls about to become clods of dirt
as if no one had ever rested their back there.
Did my mother bathe before bed or early in the morning?
Did she leave her hair in the comb's teeth to ward off

الحسد؟ من النار؟ من شرّ الجارات؟
شعر أمي يطلع كهدية، كعقاب،
أيّة علاقة تجمعنا الآن؟
أعطيتُ فساتينها صدقةً لأنها لا تناسبني،
ولو تقابلنا الآن فسأبدو لها مثل أختٍ كبرى.
أيّة علاقة ورحمها كان قد دُفن معها، هناك،
تحت شجرة كافور حيث الموت المبكر قريب من اليد.

the evil eye, or fire, or the stratagems of neighbors?
My mother's hair glistens like a gift, or retribution.
What ties me to her now?
I donated her dresses because they weren't my style.
If we met I'd be her older sister.
What ties me to her now that her womb is in the ground with her—there
under the camphor tree, where early death is close enough to touch
    with your hand?

Translated by Robyn Creswell

الشرّ

كنت أظن أن هناك شراً كثيراً في العالم
فرغم أنني أكثر أصدقائي حناناً، لم أر وردةً على مائدة
إلا وطحنتُ طرّفها بين الإبهام والسبّابة
لأتأكّد أنها ليست من البلاستيك.

مؤخراً بدأت أشك في وجود الشرّ أصلاً
كأنّ الأذى كله يكون قد حدث بالفعل
في اللحظة التي نتأكد فيها
أن الكائنات التي أدميْنها كانت حقيقية.

Evil

There must be so much evil in the world,
I'd thought. You see,
Though I'm the gentlest of my friends,
I never saw a rose upon a table
Without crushing the petal's edge,
Thumb and finger making sure
It wasn't plastic.

Lately, I've come to doubt that evil is at all
Like all the harm already has been done
That instant when we see for sure
What we make bleed is real.

Translated by Robin Moger

الطيران

رأسي على كتفك،

لا بدّ أن المضيفة ظنت أننا ذاهبان لشهر عسل

من غرب المحيط إلى شرقه، نومٌ آمن بشهرٍ منكوشٍ

ويدين مضمومتين على الصدر،

وكتفك وسادتي.

أنت شربت كل هذا النبيذ بحذرٍ حتى لا توقظ امرأةً لا تعرف اسمها.

لن أخبرك أنني صحّحت عشرين بحثاً عن الأدب ما بعد الكولونيالي وطبختُ

طعاماً يكفي طفلين لمدة أسبوع ولففتُ والتر بنيامين حتى أحميه في ملابسي

الداخلية ولم أنس الكمبيوتر ولا شاحن الكاميرا ولا المسودّات

وكل ذلك مما يحرق الأعصاب حتى أنني نمتُ على كتف رجل لا أعرف اسمه.

لا بدّ أننا شبيهان، حياةُ كلٍّ منّا كثيرة ولكنها تبدو في لحظةٍ كهذه بلا تاريخ

ولا مستقبل، مثل زجاجة صغيرة من المياة تشربها على عجلٍ ثم تلقيها في أول

سلّة مهملات.

Flying

my head on your shoulder

the stewardess had to think that we were on our honeymoon

from the west coast of the ocean to its east: a sleep
secure with tousled hair
hands pressed to chest

your shoulder my pillow

you drinking all this wine,
so careful not to wake a woman whose name you do not know

I don't tell you that I have corrected twenty essays on post-
colonial literature and made enough food to feed two boys for
a week and wrapped up Walter Benjamin in my underwear to

لا تسألني عن مكان الوصول، لمجرد أنك تركت لي كتفك لخمس ساعات أو لأنك لم تذهب بسببي للحمّام، ربما لم أكن غائبة تماماً.

keep him safe and brought (and not forgotten) the computer
and the charger for the camera and the drafts & all that
fraying on my nerves so I can sleep upon the shoulder of a man
whose name I do not know

we must be similar, so much in both our lives. but in moments
such as this they seem to have no history, no future, a bottle of
water drunk down and thrown into the nearest bin

don't ask me where we're coming to. just by lending me your
shoulder for five hours, not going to the bathroom because of
me, perhaps I was not completely absent

Translated by Robin Moger

رسّام الملائكة

تترك الألوان الحقودة خارج اللوحة، تدّعي الروحانية فلا تقترح صوتاً ولا رائحة. أجسادٌ بيضاء ووجوهٌ هلامية، أجنحةٌ تلتصق بالورقة كوشم ولن تطير أبداً.

الكائنات التي ترسمها ملائكة بامتياز، ولم يرها أيٌ من زبائنك حتى يُسائل موهبتك.

Painter of angels

Leave spiteful colors off your canvas. Assert the spiritual: propose no sound or smell. White bodies, jelly faces. Wings are pasted to the fabric like tattoos and will never fly. What you paint are perfect angels. None of your customers have ever seen one. They cannot call your gift into question.

Translated by Robin Moger

مثل القصيدة التي كنت أكتبها في آلحلم

غريمي على ركبتيه وجمهوره يصرخ " كيف لن يقتل أحدٌ أحداً "
معجزاتٌ تحدث ولا تسأل كيف
السيفُ تحت إبطي مثل شمسية تنتظر مطراً لتنفتح وترخّ السماءُ حروفاً
كلّما تكوّنت كلمة التأم جرحٌ ما في هذا العالم
في الطريق كأنني كنت على طرف قناة وأمي على الطرف الآخر
بيننا سرب من الأَوَزّ نجحنا أخيراً في إعادتها إلى البيت
في البيت كنت أقشّر برتقالاً وأقطّع تفاحاً في جلسة
صلحٌ مع الفاكهة
وكأن عيالي أكلوا كثيراً حتى أنني خفتُ أن أحسدهم
ربما نمتُ بعدها
وكانت لذة تصحو في أصابع قدميّ
الدم كان نظيفاً في عروقي
وتؤرجحني سحابة

Like the poem I was writing in the dream

My enemy on his knees, mob shouting, How come
No one is going to kill anyone?
Miracles happen and you don't ask how come?
Sword under my arm, an umbrella
Waiting for rains to open, for the sky to rain letters.
Whenever a word is formed a wound in this world is somewhere sealed.
On the path, like
Me on one side of an irrigation ditch, my mother on the other,
Between us a flock of geese that we bring home at last.
At home I was peeling oranges and cutting apples
In a truce with fruit. Like,
My children ate so much I was afraid even to envy them.
Maybe later I slept,
Then a thrill waking in my toes
And the blood clean in my veins
And a cloud rocking me.

السعادة اكتملت

والغريب أنني عرفت لحظتها أنها السعادة.

Happiness made complete and strangely I knew
In the moment it was happiness.

Translated by Robin Moger

Mohamad Nassereddine

Lebanon

TRANSLATED BY HUDA FAKHREDDINE

حبل الغسيل

لا أعرف البتّة
إن كان الأمر طريقةً
لتجفيف الدموع:
امرأة لساعة كاملة
تثبّت عينيها
في حبل غسيلٍ تحت الشمس.

Clothesline

I have no idea
if this was a way
to dry her tears:
For an hour,
the woman fixes her eyes
on the clothesline in the sun.

هرطقة الميكانيكي

الميكانيكيّ بالثوب الأزرق
حين يحدّق في السماء
يظنّ لبرهة أنّه الرب
هو أيضا يحمل أفكاراً نظيفة
ويدين ملطختين.

The Mechanic's Heresy

When the mechanic in blue
stares up at the sky,
for a minute, he thinks himself God.
He too has clean thoughts
and soiled hands.

الكلاب

أريدُ أن أكتب لك
قصيدة في الحب
أبحث في اللغة
عن مفردة رقيقة
تصطفّ الكلمات كالكلاب المدرّبة
تنطلق باحثة عن الديناميت
تتّجه بأسنانها نحو قلبي.

Dogs

I want to write you
a love poem.
I search in language
for a tender word.
But words line up like trained dogs
and spread out in search of dynamite,
their teeth aimed
at my heart.

Saadiah Mufarreh

Kuwait

TRANSLATED BY ALLISON BLECKER

تَواضَعتْ أَحلامي كَثيراً

1

أُريدُ مُجرَّدَ جناحين
أو يَكُفُّ روحي عن تَوْقِه للطَيَران.

2

أُريدُ أنْ أصرُخَ كُلَّ صَرْخَتي
من دون أنْ أنْتظرَ سُؤالاً ما.

3

أُريدُ أنْ أتخلَّص من كُلِّ ما يُعيق دَمْعتي
عن هدَفِها المُؤَجَّل
أوْ نُقْطتِها الأخيرة على السَّطرِ.

4

أُريدُ أنْ أغنّي
من دون أنْ أُضطر لتأليفِ كلامٍ

64

My Dreams Often
Humble Themselves

1

I want nothing more than wings
or my soul to cease yearning for flight.

2

I want to cry out with all my might
without waiting for any question.

3

I want to free myself from everything that keeps my tears
from their deferred goal
or their final dot on the line.

4

I want to sing
without being obliged to compose words,

أَوْ أَرْتجِلَ لَحَناً
أَوْ أَرفعَ صَوتي.

5

أُريدُ كُرَةً أَرضيةً
أَرسُمُ خريطَتَها
وفقاً لتضاريسِ وجْهي
وأشُقُّ أَنهارَها وبِحارَها
على طريقِ دمْعتي.

6

أُريدُ كُرَةً أَرضيَّةً أُخرى
أَخَبِّئُها في صَدْري
كُلَّما أَرَدْتُ الخُروجَ من البيتِ
من دون عباءةٍ.

7

أُريدُ شَجَرةً تُغنّي
وعصفورةً تُهادنُ الريحَ
وبحْراً يكتُبُ مُذكّراتِهِ كُلَّ فجْر
وجوازَ سَفَرٍ صالِحاً في كُلِّ المطاراتِ.

8

أُريدُ مظلَّةً مُزيَّنةً بِقرنفلةٍ

66

improvise a tune,
or raise my voice.

5

I want an earth
whose map I can draw
in accordance with the topography of my face,
cleaving its rivers and seas
by way of my tears.

6

I want another earth
I can conceal in my chest
whenever I want to leave the house
without an abaya.

7

I want a tree that sings,
a sparrow that makes a truce with the wind,
a sea that writes its memoirs each dawn,
and a passport that is accepted at all airports.

8

I want an umbrella adorned with a carnation,

وكتاباً مَفتوحاً على الفهرس
وأصابعَ تُجيدُ نَقرَ لَوْحةِ المفاتيح.

9

أُريدُ مُجرّد مخدَّةٍ مُريحةٍ
وأَحْلاماً تَسيرُ أَحداثُها
وفقاً لسيناريوهاتي المرسومةِ سَلَفاً.

10

أُريدُ حكايةً قديمةً بنهايةٍ سعيدةٍ
أَحْكيها للصغار
وأُشيرُ لصُوَرِ أَبْطَالِها في أَلْبوم العائلة.

11

أُريدُ مُجرّدَ إطارٍ بسيطٍ وجميلٍ
للوحةٍ بدائيةٍ رسَمْتُها بالقلمِ الرصاصِ
ولوّنتُها بالألوانِ الخشبيّةِ...
كيْ أُهْديها لصديقتي البعيدة.

12

أُريدُ أَنْ تَتَّسِعَ غُرْفَتي
لتَحْتوي كُلَّ كُتبي الكثيرة
أو تُصيبني نوبةُ جُنونٍ
فأَحْرق هذه الكتب.

a book open to the index,
and fingers skilled at tapping on the keyboard.

9

I want nothing more than a comfortable pillow
and dreams whose events unfold
in accordance with scenarios written in advance.

10

I want an old story with a happy ending
to tell to the children
while pointing at pictures of its heroes in the family album.

11

I want nothing more than a simple, beautiful frame
for a primitive picture I drew in graphite
and colored pencils
to give to a distant friend.

12

I want my room to expand
to contain all my many books
or for a fit of madness to strike me
so I will burn them.

13

أُريدُ ذكرى حلوةً
ويَقيناً شِعريّاً...
ونَهاراً جديداً.

14

أُريدُ كِسْرَةَ "عُود"
أضَعُها على جَمْرةٍ مُتَوقّدةٍ
فيَفوحُ العَبَقُ المُعطَّرُ
بينما أشربُ قَهوتي الصباحيَّة
من دون أفكارٍ مُسبقةٍ
لِبقيّةِ النهار.

15

أُريدُ غوايةً جَديدةً
لأيامٍ فَقط...

16

أُريدُ فيلماً بالأسودِ والأبيضِ
أغنّي مع بَطَلتهِ
أتَخَيَّلُني بِكنْزَتِها الضيقةِ
وتَنُّورتِها الفَضْفاضةِ
أمْسَحُ دَمعَتَها
وأضْحَكُ على سذاجَتِها

13

I want a sweet memory,
a poetic certainty,
and a new day.

14

I want a sliver of incense
to put on a burning ember
so the perfumed fragrance will spread
while I drink my morning coffee
without giving prior thought
to the rest of the day.

15

I want a new temptation
only for a few days.

16

I want a black-and-white film
whose heroine I can sing along with;
I imagine myself in her tight pullover
and flowing skirt,
wipe away her tears,
and laugh at her naïveté,

حتى أُبَرِّرَ سذاجاتِ تاريخي كُلِّه.

17

أُريدُ أغنيةً هادئةً
لليلٍ ساهرة عيونه.

18

أُريدُ نهاراً طويلاً ومُزدحماً
برائحةِ البحرِ والرملِ
وعوادم السياراتِ
وبقليلٍ من المكالماتِ المفقودةِ
في هاتفي النقالِ.

19

أُريدُ نهاراً قصيراً جداً
يَكفي لِكتابةِ قَصيدةٍ
أكتُبها كما أشتهي
على مَهلٍ
من دون رُتوشٍ
ولا مُسودةٍ.

20

أُريدُ لَيلاً قصيراً
مُؤَطَّراً بالهدوءِ

until I justify all of the naiveties of my past.

17
I want a soft song
for a night with eyes wide awake.

18
I want a long, full day,
with the smell of the sand and sea,
car exhaust,
and fewer missed calls
on my cellphone.

19
I want a very short day,
enough for writing a poem,
composed as I desire,
leisurely,
unadorned,
and without a draft.

20
I want a short night
framed in tranquility,

يَنْتهي بموتٍ
لا يَعني أَحَداً...

21

أُريدُ ليلاً طويلاً
أعْني طويلاً جداً.

22

أُريدُ أنْ أحْيا
من دونِ أنْ يكونَ ذلك قَدَري الأَزَليّ
حينَ تَعِزُّ الخياراتُ.

23

أُريدُ أنْ أموتَ
من دون أنْ أضطَرَّ لذلك
أَحْياناً...

24

أُريدُهُ فقط
ما هوَ؟
منْ هوَ؟
لا أُريدُ الإجابةَ على أيةِ حالٍ.

ending with a death
that concerns no one.

21

I want a long night,
I mean truly long.

22

I want to live
without that being my eternal fate
when alternatives are scarce.

23

Sometimes
I want to die
without having to do so.

24

I want only it.
What is it?
Who is it?
I don't want an answer in any case.

25

"لنا الصَّدرُ دون العالمينَ...
أو القبرُ"
نَعَمْ...
لهذا المتواضِع كُلُ الصُّدورِ حَتماً
وليَترُكَ لي قبراً
بنافِذةٍ واحِدةٍ على الأقلِ!

25

"We are on the front line, first among the peoples of the world,
   or we are in the grave."
Yes,
all of the honor is inevitably for this modest man;
let him leave me a grave
with at least one window!

Riyad al-Salih al-Hussein

Syria

Translated by Rana Issa
and Suneela Mubayi

العصر
النيترو

مارسيليز العصر النيتروني

في عصر الحب البلاستيكي والقلوب البلاستيكية
ثمة قطارات تذهب بالجنود إلى الموت في الأعياد
وثمة مهرجون يبكون على أنفسهم سرًّا
ويُضحكون الآخرين على الحلبة
في عصر المدافئ الغازية والاختناق بالغاز
أشمُّ أصابع حبيبتي
وأشرب ذكرياتها البليدة
هذه الفتاة تثرثر كثيرًا عن الحقول
وتجمع صور الأطفال
كهاوية طوابع محترفة
حتى أنها لا تستطيع أن تقتنع
بأن الأمهات سيكففن عن الإنجاب
لأننا نعيش في العصر النيتروني

***

إننا نعيش في العصر النيتروني
عصر القبلات السريعة في الشوارع
والاندحار الفادح في الشوارع أيضًا

80

A Marseillaise for the Neutron Age

In the age of plastic love and plastic hearts
There are trains that take soldiers to death during holidays
And some clowns that weep for themselves secretly
And make others laugh in the ring
In the epoch of gas heaters and gas asphyxiation
I smell my lover's fingers
And drink her dull memories
This girl goes on about fields
And collects pictures of children
Like a professional stamp collector
She cannot even be convinced
That mothers will stop giving birth
Because we live in the neutron age
***
We live in the neutron age
The age of quick kisses in the streets
And being utterly vanquished in the streets

إننا نعيش عصرنا الضاري
عصر الجواسيس الذين يقدمون لك القهوة
مع المورفين
عصر الطائرات التي تطعم البشر القنابل
والألعاب
إنه عصرنا النيتروني
عصر الأحذية المثقوبة والكلابات
عصر التعب البطيء
من الساعة (صفر) حتى الساعة الخامسة والعشرين
ومن عصرنا النيتروني
عصرنا ما قبل الأخير
ندعوكم: تعالوا...
أيها البرجوازيون التعساء
تعالوا وشاركونا النحيب والسجون والأغاني

***

وهنالك قيد واحد وهناك أغانٍ تتربة
وهنالك أسرّة بعدد العشاق
و توابيت بعدد اللصوص
وهنا... هنا
رجل معتم وامرأة معتمة و سبعة عيدان من الكبريت
عود كبريت واحد يكفي:
لإضاءة شمعة
أم لتفجير مدينة؟
عود كبريت واحد يكفي:

We live our ferocious age
The age of spies that serve you coffee
With morphine
The age of planes that feed bombs and toys
To humans
It's our neutron age
The age of tattered shoes and clamps
The age of slow exhaustion
From 00:00 hours to 25:00 hours
From our neutron age
Our penultimate age
We invite you—come
You wretched bourgeoisie
Come and share in the wailing, the prisons, and the songs
***
There is one handcuff and Tartar songs
And there are as many beds as lovers
And as many coffins as thieves
And Here...
Here is an unlit man, an unlit woman, and seven matchsticks
Is one matchstick enough
To light a candle
Or blow up a city?
Is one matchstick enough

لتحضير كأسين من الشاي

أم لتحضير محرقة للملحدين؟

عود كبريت واحد يكفي:

لتنظيف الأسنان

أم لإخفاء معالم جثة مغتصبة؟

وهنا... هنا

حتى الموتى يمكن أن يتألموا

وحتى الموتى يمكن أن يتقنوا الرقص

وحتى الموتى يمكن أن يتلوثوا

إننا ملوّثون للغاية

ملوّثون بالحروب وملوّثون بالمجاعات

نحن الموتى الموسميون:

شرابيننا محقونة بالضجيج و مقابرنا

محقونة بالدخان

نحن العشاق الموسميون:

قلوبنا ملطخة بالأرق وليالينا ملطخة بالآهات

نحن العمال الموسميون:

مرهقون دائمًا وليس أبدًا

مرهقون منذ الأهرامات وحتى جوهرة

بوكاسا الفريدة

***

في عصر الرؤوس المفلطحة

ومصانع الحب التكنيكي

وأرغفة الجوع الفاتك

To make two cups of tea
Or plan a holocaust for atheists?
Is one matchstick enough
To pick teeth
Or to hide the traces of a violated corpse?
Here...
Here even the dead can be in pain
Even the dead can become perfect dancers
Even the dead can get contaminated
We are utterly contaminated
Contaminated with war and famine
We are the seasonal dead:
Our veins are injected with commotion and our cemeteries
Injected with smoke
We are the seasonal lovers:
Our hearts smeared with insomnia and our nights with cries
We are seasonal workers
Constantly exhausted but never forever
We have been exhausted since the pyramids and
Until Bokassa's rare jewels
***
In the age of flatheads
And the factories of mechanized love
And the loaves of deadly hunger

في زمننا الحقيقي الاسطوري هذا
نخرج إليكم... نخرج إليكم
لا من القبور ولا من المحيطات
لا من الكتب ولا من الجدران
نخرج إليكم... نخرج إليكم
وبأيدينا كل شيء...
بأيدينا القمصان الملطخة بالزيوت والطين
بأيدينا مساحيق الـ د. د. ت
شفرات الناسيت الحادة
انتظارنا العادل ودساتيركم البارعة
نخرج إليكم... نخرج إليكم
لسنا أشرارًا ولا مهذبين
لا نحب العنف ولا نكره الطيور
وأجسادنا تفوح دائمًا برائحة المعادن واليانسون
نخرج إليكم... نخرج إليكم
بشرفاتنا وأيامنا التي تتساقط كالذباب
بزمننا المعطوب
ببيوتنا المعطوبة
بأجسادنا المعطوبة
بأحلامنا المعطوبة وفاكهتنا المعطوبة
نخرج إليكم... نخرج إليكم
نحن مواطنو العصر النيتروني
عصر الرؤوس المزروعة بالألغام
والقلوب الطافحة بالأغاني

In this real-mythical age of ours
We come out, out to meet you
Not from cemeteries or oceans
Not from books, not from walls
We come out to meet you—
With everything in our hands...
Shirts that are smeared with oil and mud
DDT powder
Nacet razor blades
Our legitimate waiting and your expert constitutions
We come out, out to meet you
We are neither evil nor polite
We neither like violence nor do we hate birds
And our bodies always smell of metal and anise
We come out, out to meet you
With our balconies and days that drop like flies
With our damaged age
With our damaged homes
Our damaged bodies
Our damaged dreams and our damaged fruit
We come out, out to meet you
We, the citizens of the neutron age
The age of heads planted with landmines
And hearts overflowing with song

***

إنه عصرنا النيتروني
عصر المساطر و المرائي والدبابات
إنه عصرنا النيتروني
عصر الشجر النووي والعصافير النازية
والإذاعات وعصر المواعيد الفتية:
مع المدافن نهار السبت
مع الحزن نهار الأحد
مع الخنازير نهار الإثنين
مع الجنون نهار الثلاثاء
مع الرشيشات نهار الأربعاء
ومع الموت الوسيم
إنه عصر المواعيد الفتية الخائنة في جميع الليالي
وفي جميع الليالي
في جميع الليالي
لكِ موعد مع قلبي.

***

It is our neutron age
The age of scales, eulogies, and tanks
It is our neutron age
The age of nuclear trees and Nazi sparrows
Of radio broadcasts
And the age of youthful dating:
With Saturday burials
And sadness on Sunday
With pigs on Monday
And madness on Tuesday
With machine guns on Wednesday
And handsome death
It is the age of youthful dating, scared all night
Every night
And every night
You have a date
With my heart

Ines Abassi

Tunisia

TRANSLATED BY KOEN DE CUYPER
AND HODNA BENTALI GHARSALLAH NUERNBERG

والبيت

المفتاح

آخر مفتاح حملتُه معي،
يتدلى وحيدا من علّاقة المفاتيح
مثل جسد مشنوق في العراء
مفتاح البيت الذي لم يعد بيتنا
الذي لن يكون بيتنا بعد اليوم
يعلوه صدأ الذكريات
وغبار الصحراء التي خلفناها وراءنا
والبيت؟
ربما ستعيد طلاء جدرانه التي تشرّبت صراخنا
وعرق كلماتنا المُتعبة
الكلمات... كم تشظّت بيننا
وحجبت الضوء المشّع بالألوان
ظهرك عار ويدي عارية
الضوء يفصل بيننا
الأفكار تفصل بيننا
الباب لا يفصل بيننا
الطرقات لا تفصل بيننا

The Key

The last key I carried
dangles alone on the key rack
like a corpse at the gallows
the key to the house that is no longer our house
that won't be our house tomorrow
is rusted with memories
and coated with the desert sand we left in our wake
and the house?
maybe the walls that soaked up our screams
and the sweat of our tired words
will repaint themselves
our words so often splintered
veiling the radiant light with colors
your back is naked, my hand is naked
light separates us
ideas separate us
it's not the door

أما ظهرك العاري... فيفصل بيننا
احتجت لدموع وقصائد كثيرة
قصائد أخريات علّمت أيامهن كدمات زرقاء
احتجت للغصة التي علّمت قلبي بكدمة سوداء
احتجت لكلّ كلماتنا المختنقة
بهواء الغرفة الفاسد، الثقيل بأنفاسنا
الثقيل بالغضب والكثير من الكذب
أنشوطة الأكاذيب ضفرتَها أنت
وفككتُها أنا
بصبر امرأة أعماها الحب سنواتٍ
مفتاح البيت الذي لم يعد بيتنا
الذي لن يكون بيتنا بعد اليوم
ألقيت به مع كراكيب الذكريات.

nor the roads
but your naked back that separates us
I needed tears and many poems,
other poems whose days bruised them blue
I needed anguish to bruise my heart black
I needed all our choked words
and the sour air heavy with our breaths
heavy with anger and all the lies
a tress of lies you braided
I undid it
with the patience of a woman long blinded by love
the key to the house that is no longer our house
that won't be our house tomorrow
I threw it out with a heap of memories

وشم

في حياة أخرى... قريبا
ربما بعد الاربعين
سأحصل على "تاتو"
وشم... بالعربية
الكلمة أكثر أناقة بالعربية
سأقلب دفتر الصور ببطء ودلال
قد أختار
وشم العقرب التي لم أكنها
أو وشم أفعى
أو حتى وشما لعنكبوت
يمكنني أيضا اختيار كلمة
قد تتغرز الإبرة في لحمي
بكلمة مثل
"خيانة"
أو
"لامبالاة"
اللامبالاة كلمة أكبر من الخيانة

Tattoo

In another life, one that's not so far off
(maybe after forty)
I'd get a tattoo
washm, in Arabic
the word is more elegant in Arabic
I'd page through the album slowly, delicately
I'd choose
a tattoo of the scorpion that I wasn't
or a tattoo of a snake
or even a tattoo of a spider
or I'd choose a word
the needle etching into my skin
a word like
betrayal
or
indifference
indifference is a bigger word than *betrayal*

كلمة أطول
تحتاج لمساحة أكبر
سأنسى تماما فكرتي عن مقايضة الملح بالكتب
على أبواب تمبكتو
كان هذا حلما قديما لحياة أقدم
طالما حلمتُ بها
سأنسى بأنه كان من الممكن لي
في حياة أخرى
في تمبكتو
كان من الممكن أن أكون في غرفة باردة
يحيط بي الحرير والخيال والصحبة الطيّبة
لكنني هنا الآن اليوم
في هذا الزمن
أريد بنطال جينز ممزقا عند الركبتين
وقميصا أبيض
ضاعت نصف أزراره العلوية

ورغم أنني أريد
تعلم العزف على جيتار الكتروني
إلا أنني...
لا أريد أساور جلدية حول معصمي
أريد فقط أن أتعلم عزف
موسيقى تكسر زجاج النوافذ
وتفتت الألم...

a longer word
you need more space
I'd utterly forget my idea of trading salt for books
at the gates of Timbuktu
it was the old dream of an even older life
I long dreamed of it
I'd forget I ever considered it possible
in another life
in Timbuktu
I could have been in a cool room
surrounded by silk, imagination, and good company
but I'm here now
and right now
I want jeans with ripped knees
and a white shirt
with half the buttons undone

and although I want
to learn to play the electric guitar
I don't want leather bracelets on my wrists
I only want to learn to play
music that breaks windows
and shatters pain
I want to play my pain

أريد أن أعزف ألمي
أن أصرخ بألمي
جرحي
مثل الصدع الافريقي...
ممتد طويلا في عمق الأرض
ولا يلتئم
ربما... موسيقى بكل هذا الصخب
قد تكسر الزجاج حول روحي...
وتفتت ألمي.

shout my pain
my wound
like the East African Rift
plunging deep into the earth
it won't heal
maybe music in all of its noise
will break the glass around my soul
and shatter my pain

دانتيلا

إلى ج.ف.

الليلُ لنا
والليل نهرٌ نعبرُه
عاشقان غريبان نحنُ
كلما تشابكت أصابعنا، افترقنا
يفصل بيننا الوقت والبحر الأبيض المتوسّط
ولا قارب للعبور سوى الحب

آخر ليلة قبل الرحيل،
لم نتكلم
ولا حتى بلغة الأصابع
آخر ليلة،
تقاسمنا في صمت سيجارا كوبيا
بينما غلفتنا رائحة الخريف
كانت الحرارة تسع درجات
وحرارةُ قلبي كانت بحرارة بركان
تذوقتَ عسل الكستناء على شفتيّ
تذوقتُ فانيليا "الروم" على شفتيكَ

Lace

for JF

the night is ours
the night is a river we cross
two strange lovers
when our fingers interlaced, we parted ways
we are separated by time and the Mediterranean
no boat to cross it but love

the last night before leaving
we didn't speak
not even the language of fingers
that last night
we shared a Cuban cigar in silence
as the odor of autumn enveloped us
it was nine degrees out
but my heart was a volcano
my lips tasted of chestnut honey
and yours of vanilla rum

آخر ليلة،
رقصنا ببطء وصمت في الشرفة
بينما انهمر المطرُ فوقنا
خفيفا وناعما مثل الحزن... كان المطرُ
آخر ليلة قبل الرحيل،
لم نتكلم كثيراً

وكلما تكلمتَ
علقت لغتي على شفتيك
أرسم لك في الهواء الحروف
فتدهشك الشدّة والضمّة والحروف المنقطة
"العين" حرفٌ مُدور يعلق في حلقك
فتضمّني إليك ونسكت.

**

آخر ليلة
كان الليل نهرا
لم أرَ وجهي في عتمة ماءه
لفنا الليل
برائحة الأرض إذْ يُبلّلها المطر
برائحة الرغبة
إذْ ترتفعُ في ليل الريف الفرنسيّ

that last night
we slow danced on the balcony in silence
as it rained down on us
rain as light and soft as sorrow
that last night before leaving
we barely spoke

but when you did
my language hung on your lips
I traced the letters in the air for you
the *shadda*, the *damma*, and the dotted letters startled you
the '*ayn* is a rounded letter that lingers in your throat
I embraced you in silence

**

that last night
night became a river
I couldn't make out my face in the darkness of the water
the night wrapped us up
in the smell of earth wet from the rain
and the smell of desire
that rose in the darkness of the French countryside

كل مرّة
ترتفع رائحتنا... رائحة رغبتنا
متوحشة
بريّة
رائعة
قبل الليلة الأخيرة عبرنا معا طرقات العنب
صعودا
عبرنا نحو مدينة بلون النبيذ
"بُوردو"... مدينة حبنا
بوردو مثل حبنا
مثل زهرة برتقال متفتحة
نحن العاشقان الذين التقيا خلف الشاشات
وتبادلا "الرسائل الالكترونية" بصبر
وحين التقينا أخيرا
أيقظنا معا بضع صباحات بصفير آلة القهوة،
وختمنا ليلنا بأغنية المطر والعسل و "الروم" والسيجار،
أنت العاشق الذي
يسقط منك حرف الحاء
كلما قلت أحبك...

ويتشكل خاءا
تُكرر: "أخبكِ"
مرّة بعد مرّة
بينما يمتد الليلُ فوقنا مثل دانتيلا سوداء

106

every time
this fragrance of ours fills the air, the odor of our desire
wild
savage
thrumming
before that last night we walked through vineyards
sloping toward
Bordeaux, a city the color of wine
the city of our love
like an orange flower in bloom
we are lovers who meet behind screens
sending endless emails
and when we finally met
the whistling coffee pot woke us up
and we fell asleep to songs, rain, honey, rum, and cigars
you are the lover who
drops the letter *ha*
every time you say *uhibuki*, I love you

it comes out as a *kha*
you repeated *ukhibuki*
over and over
while the night stretched out above us like black lace
you sighed and said Arabic is a difficult language

لتتنهد قائلا: "العربية لغة صعبة
لكنني 'أخبك'، يا امرأتي العربيّة"

**

أتطلع عبر النافذة
لسنا معا...
مرّة أخرى
يوم آخر يفصلنا
وبحر أبيض متوسّط، يفصلنا
بينما دانتيلا الليل تعرشُ على جسدي
برغبة وحنين.

but ukhibuki, my Arab love

**

I glance out the window
we're not together
and once again
another day separates us
the Mediterranean separates us
as the lace of night drapes my body
with aching desire

Ahmed Shafie

Egypt

Translated by Hodna Bentali Gharsallah Nuernberg
and Ahmed Shafie

في الموضع الذي فيه للناس ذاكرةٌ
لي أنا ذراعان،
لا أدري
لرقصة هما منفتحان
أم لعناق

هكذا يبقى لي من القرية البعيدة
أن فيها حيوانات وأقارب
وحكايات حتى عن الموتى
وليس إلا نمائم
عن الراحلين.

1

Where most people have memories
I have two arms
held wide open
inviting a dance
or offering an embrace.

And so,
all I have left of that distant village is:
There are animals, relatives,
tales of the dead,
and gossip.
Nothing but gossip
about the ones who left.

حبيبتي التي كلما خطت
إلى الكنيسة
خطوةً
خطوةً
تراجعت الكنيسة

حبيبتي
التي تعرف الكنيسة أنها
ما لها
أن تعبد أحدا.

2

My sweetheart,
who steps toward the church
and the church always
steps back

My sweetheart,
who the church clearly knows
shouldn't
worship anyone.

3

تذكروا يا أصدقائي النبلاء
وأنت تحررون الوطن
أن تتركوا قطعةً صغيرة منه،
قطعةً صغيرة جدا
لن تعوق بناء أقواس النصر،
لكنها ستكفي تماما
لكي لا تتوه عن الوطن
روح أبي.

3

Remember, my noble friends:
When you liberate our fatherland
leave one small fraction of it,
a very little piece,
unliberated.
It won't hinder the construction
of your triumphal arches,
but it'll be enough
for my own father's soul
to find its way home.

4

بين حين وآخر
يودعني غرابُ قلبَه
ويأخذ قلبي.

بقلب صغير،
هو قلب طائر في النهاية،
لا يستطيع المرء أن يحب
ولو طائراً صغيرا

ثم إنه يعود ليأخذ قلبه
فيجده عرقان
ساخنا
يلهث
كأنه هو أيضا
كان يطير.

4

Every now and then
the raven entrusts his heart
to me
and takes mine in return.

With a small heart,
a bird's heart after all,
you cannot love
even a little bird.

And when he returns
to reclaim his heart,
he finds it sweating
hot
gasping
as if it, too,
were flying.

Ashjan Hendi

Saudi Arabia

Translated by Moneera Al-Ghadeer

لا تنمو

شمسلا

أصفر!

أيُّها الرجل الغاضبُ
ذو الوجهِ الأصفر الشاحبْ:
ما الذي يجعلكَ تغارُ من زهرة عبّاد الشمسِ؟!
غير جمالِها؟
واكتمالِها؟
ما الذي يُزعجكَ أيضًا
استدارتِها الفاتنة،
وغير طولِها،
وقامتها العالية،
ما الذي يزعجكَ أيضًا
غير لونها
وغير أنها:
لا تنمو باتجاه شمسك؟!

Sallow

Hey, angry man
with your sallow face:
what makes you jealous of the sunflower
but her allure?
Her lavishness?
What else irritates you?

Other than her sensual petals,
her highness
and dignity?
What else irritates you
but her colors
and that
she doesn't lean toward your sun?

في أواخر ديسمبر

لا تعشق حتى الثمالة؛
فهذه آخر زجاجة حب
على طاولة هذا العام:
أعد الثمالة إلى الكأس،
والكأس إلى الزجاجة،
والزجاجة إلى العنب،
والعنب إلى الكرم،
والعشق إلى العاشق،
وعقارب الزمن إلى ساعة الحائط،
أدر كرسيك الأوحد
عكس عقارب الساعة،
ثم أعد ترتيب الطاولة.

End of December

Refrain from being drunk
in love. Don't drink
love's last bottle
from this year's table.
Return the dregs to your glass,
the glass back to full bottle.
Return the bottle to its grapes,
the grapes to the vineyard,
love back to its lover.
Return Time's movement
and Time's dial
back to the clock on the wall.
Turn your lone chair
counterclockwise,
then reset the table.

قوارير

حين كنت أغني:
كانوا يجمعون صوتي في زجاجة،
يلقونها في غياهب الوقت؛
فتلتقطها عرائس البحر...

وحين كانت عرائس البحر تغني:
كانوا يكسرون عنق الزجاجة،
يلقونها في أعماق الصمت؛
هكذا ابتلعت أسماك القرش صوتي،
وصوت عرائس البحر...

Bottles

While I was singing,
they stopped my voice inside
a bottle,
threw it into the depths of time
for the mermaids to catch.
When the mermaids sang,
they broke the bottle's neck,
tossed it into fathomless silence
so the sharks would swallow my voice,
then that of the mermaids.

Fadhil al-Azzawi

Iraq

TRANSLATED BY WILLIAM M. HUTCHINS

الرجل المجهول

أبداً نترُك أياماً
نقذفُها في بئر
مثل حصاة
تسقط في لَيل.
أبداً يخرجُ مُبتلاً رجلٌ مجهولٌ
يجلسُ عند الفوهة
ويُعيدُ لنا ما ضاع.

The Unknown Man

We always leave our days behind us.
We drop them in a well
Like a pebble
Falling in the night.
A wet, unknown man always climbs up,
Sits on the wellhead,
And gives us back
What we have lost.

عائداً من الماضي
يلتقيني، فوق كتفيهِ رجالٌ من جص
فنجلسُ معا على مقعدٍ في حديقة
ونقرأ كتابَ الحياة
على ضوءِ شمعةٍ خابية
ثم نخرجُ معا نتسكعُ في الشوارع
حتى الفجر.
عائداً من الليلِ والنهار كان يستيقظُ مبكراً
ويحلقُ ذقنَه مُغنّياً كما نفعلُ في المعتقلات
وإذ يراني نائماً يموتُ من الأمل
فأتركه للمارة وأنحدِرُ الى النهر
لأغسلَ جسدي منه
جسدي الذي سأُعَبِّئُه بالضحايا
وأمنحُه للأيام
الآنَ وفي المستقبل.

He

Returning from the past,
He meets me, with a cast of plaster men on his shoulders.
Then we sit together on a garden bench
And read the Book of Life
By the light of a dying candle.
We venture into town together, roaming the streets
Till dawn.
Returning after a night and a day,
He wakes early and
Shaves, while singing the way we did in prison camps.
Then, watching me sleep, he dies of hope.
So I leave him to the passersby and descend to the river,
To cleanse my body of him—
My body that I'll fill with victims,
And give to the passing days,
Now and in the future.

رجل في مقهى

رجلٌ
يجلسُ في زاويةٍ من مقهى
ويدخنُ في صمتٍ
بين نساءٍ مبتهجاتٍ
يتبادلن نكاتٍ لا يسمعُها
ووراء زجاج المقهى في الشارع
يخترمُ الثلجُ الأشجار
وقطاراتٌ تتوقفُ أحياناً
يصعدُ او يهبطُ منها
ركابٌ
بمعاطفَ جلدية.
رجلٌ
يجلسُ في زاويةٍ من مقهى
ينهضُ من مقعدِه
يدخلُ في معطفِه
يبحثُ عن شيءٍ ما فوق المشجب
قبعةٍ في لونِ التبنِ المحروق

A Man in a Café

A man
Sits in a corner of a café,
Smoking silently
Among joyful women, who
Exchange jokes he doesn't hear.
Outside the café's window, in the street,
Snow weighs down the trees
As trains stop occasionally,
And passengers
With leather valises
Disembark or board.
A man
Sits in a corner of a café
And then rises
To don his coat. He
Searches for something on the coat hook:
A hat the color of burnt straw

تميلُ قليلاً
نحو الأعلى
يُخفِضُها فوق جبينِه
يخرجُ للشارع
ويسيرُ
وحيداً
تحت الثلج.

With a slight
Upward tilt to the brim.
He lowers it over his brow
And ventures out to the street.
He walks
Alone
In the falling snow.

Contributors

Ines Abassi is a Tunisian writer. She has published three volumes of poetry and two collections of short stories. Her first novel appeared in 2017. From 2014 to 2016, Abassi served as the executive publisher of Dar Anahla Saghira. Her work has been translated into English, Danish, French, Korean, and Swedish.

Samer Abu Hawwash is Palestinian and was born in Lebanon in 1972. Trained as a journalist, he is a poet and translator. Abu Hawwash creates a contemporary poetic language from Arabic that breathes life into a quotidian and interior world that is haunting and ethereal. He currently resides in the UAE.

Fadhil al-Azzawi was born in Kirkuk, northern Iraq, in 1940. He has a BA in English literature from Baghdad University and a PhD in journalism from Leipzig University. He edited literary magazines and newspapers in Iraq and abroad and has been publishing his poetry since the 1960s. He left Iraq in 1977 and settled in Germany. He has published numerous volumes of poetry, six novels, one collection of short stories, two works of criticism, and many translations from English and German into Arabic. He is a contributing editor of *Banipal* magazine.

Moneera Al-Ghadeer is the author of *Desert Voices: Bedouin Women's Poetry in Saudi Arabia* (I.B. Tauris, 2009) as well as many articles, book chapters, and translations. She received her PhD from the University of California, Berkeley, and went on to become a tenured professor at the University of Wisconsin-Madison. Additionally, she was a visiting professor of comparative literature in the Department of Middle Eastern, South Asian, and African Studies at Columbia University and a Shawwaf Visiting Professor at Harvard University.

Riyad al-Salih al-Hussein (1954–1982) suffered throughout his short life from deafness, kidney failure, and diabetes. He scrounged a meager living working various menial jobs. He channeled his ailments, loves, and politics into unrhymed free verse that is at once simple and disarming. His poetry somehow foresees the devastation in Syria today.

Allison Blecker is a research associate at Swarthmore College. She received her PhD from Harvard University in Arabic literature with a secondary field in comparative literature. Her dissertation, *Eco-Alterity: Writing the Environment in the Literature of North Africa and the Middle East*, is situated at the intersection of Arabic literature and the environmental humanities. Allison's translations of Arabic poetry have appeared in *Banipal*, and she co-translated a collection of poetry by Nouri Al-Jarrah, *A Boat to Lesbos* (2018).

Robyn Creswell teaches comparative literature at Yale University. He is the translator of Abdelfattah Kilito's *The Tongue of Adam* and Sonallah Ibrahim's *That Smell and Notes from Prison* (both published by New Directions). He is the author of *City of Beginnings: Poetic Modernism in Beirut* (Princeton University Press). His essays have appeared in the *New Yorker*, the *New York Review of Books*, *The Nation*, and elsewhere.

Koen De Cuyper earned an MA in translation from the University of Leuven, during which time he spent a year in residence at the Cadi Ayyad University in Marrakech. He currently lives and works in Rabat where he is the scientific information specialist at the Netherlands Institute in Morocco (NIMAR).

Huda Fakhreddine teaches Arabic literature at the University of Pennsylvania. She is the author of *Metapoesis in the Arabic Tradition* (Brill, 2015) and the co-translator of *Lighthouse for the Drowning* (BOA editions, 2017) and *The Sky That Denied Me* (University of Texas Press, 2020). Her translations of modern Arabic poems have appeared in *Banipal, World Literature Today, Nimrod, ArabLit Quarterly,* and *Middle Eastern Literatures.*

Ashjan Hendi is a poet and scholar from Saudi Arabia. She received her PhD in Arabic literature from SOAS, University of London. Her poetry is lyrical with linguistic and figurative innovations. She received a number of poetry awards and has been translated into different languages.

William M. Hutchins has translated many works of Arabic literature into English including *Return of the Spirit* by Tawfiq al-Hakim, *The Cairo Trilogy* by Nobel Laureate Naguib Mahfouz, and *The Fetishists* by Ibrahim al-Koni. His translation of *New Waw* by al-Koni won the ALTA National Prose Translation Award for 2015. A three-time National Endowment for the Arts Fellow, Hutchins has published translations from the Arabic in *The Brooklyn Rail, Banipal, Words Without Borders,* and elsewhere.

Rana Issa is assistant professor of translation studies at the American University of Beirut and the translation editor of *Rusted Radishes* magazine. She earned her PhD at the University of Oslo and has translated theory and literature between Arabic, English, and Norwegian.

Iman Mersal is among the most celebrated contemporary poets in the Arab world, emerging from the Egyptian avant-garde movement of the 1990s. She is the author of four collections of verse and three works of prose, including *How to Mend: Motherhood and Its Ghosts*, a hybrid of cultural criticism and personal memoir. Her poetry and nonfiction work interrogate and reconstruct memory, identity, and personal history.

Robin Moger is a translator of Arabic into English. His translations of prose and poetry have appeared in *The White Review*, *Tentacular*, *Asymptote*, and *The Washington Square Review*, among others. He has translated several novels and prose works into English including Youssef Rakha's *The Crocodiles* and Iman Mersal's *How to Mend: Motherhood and Its Ghosts*. His translation of Yasser Abdel Hafez's *The Book of Safety* was awarded the 2017 Saif Ghobash Banipal Prize for Arabic Literary Translation.

Suneela Mubayi earned her PhD in Arabic literature at NYU and currently teaches Arabic literature at Cambridge University. She translates literature between Arabic, English, and Urdu, and has published in *Banipal*, *Beirut39*, *Jadaliyya*, *Words Without Borders*, and elsewhere.

Saadiah Mufarreh is a poet and critic and works as arts editor of *Al-Qabas* daily newspaper in Kuwait. She graduated from Kuwait University with a major in Arabic language and education in 1987 and has published eight collections of poetry.

Mohamad Nassereddine is a Lebanese poet born in 1977 in South Lebanon. He is the author of seven poetry collections, the most recent of which is *Aqfāṣ Tabḥath 'an 'Aṣāfīr* (Cages in search of birds) (2019). He is also a translator and a cultural journalist who regularly publishes work in the cultural appendix of the Lebanese newspaper *Al-Akhbār*.

Hodna Bentali Gharsallah Nuernberg holds an MA in francophone world studies and an MFA in literary translation, both from the University of Iowa. Her translations from the French and the Arabic have appeared in *Anomaly*, *Asymptote*, *Quarterly Literary Review Singapore*, *Poet Lore*, *Two Lines*, and elsewhere. Nuernberg lives in Morocco, where she serves as an editor-at-large for *Asymptote* and works as a translator for film and TV. Her co-translation of Raphaël Confiant's *Madam St. Clair, Queen of Harlem* was published by Diálogos in January 2020.

Ahmed Shafie is an Egyptian poet, novelist, and translator. He has published three poetry collections and two novels. His most recent collection is *77* (2017). He has translated Charles Simic, Billy Collins, Lucille Clifton, and others. Shafie blogs at http://readingtuesday.blogspot.com.

Rawad Wehbe is a PhD candidate at the University of Pennsylvania in the Department of Near Eastern Languages and Civilizations. He studies Arabic literature across historical and traditional delineations. His translations have appeared in *Inventory*, *Words Without Borders*, and *DoubleSpeak*.

Credits

Abu Hawwash, Samer. *Sīlfī Akhīra maʿa ʿĀlam Yaḥtaḍar*. Beirut: Manshūrāt al-Jamal, 2015.

al-Azzawi, Fadhil. *Fāḍil al-ʿAzzāwī: al-Aʿmāl al-Shiʿriyya*. Beirut: Manshūrāt al-Jamal, 2007.

al-Salih al-Hussein, Riyad. *al-Aʿmāl al-Kāmila: 1954-1982*. Milan: Dār al-Mutawassit, 2016.

Mersal, Iman. *Jughrāfiyā Badīla*. Cairo: Dār Sharqiyyāt, 2006. *Ḥattā Atakhallā ʿan Fikrat al-Buyūt*. Cairo: Dār Sharqiyyāt, 2013.

Mufarreh, Saadiah. *Mishyat al-Iwazzah*. Beirut: Arab Scientific Publishers; Kuwait: Dār Masmā, 2009.

Nassereddine, Mohamad. *Aqfāṣ Tabḥath ʿan ʿAṣāfīr*. Beirut: Dār al-Nahda al-ʿArabiyya, 2019.